"This series is a tremendous resource for those ⟨
understanding of how the gospel is woven thr⟨
pastors and scholars doing gospel business from ⟨
logical feast preparing God's people to apply the entire Bible to all of life with heart and mind
wholly committed to Christ's priorities."

BRYAN CHAPELL, President Emeritus, Covenant Theological Seminary; Senior Pastor, Grace Presbyterian Church, Peoria, Illinois

"Mark Twain may have smiled when he wrote to a friend, 'I didn't have time to write you a short letter, so I wrote you a long letter.' But the truth of Twain's remark remains serious and universal, because well-reasoned, compact writing requires extra time and extra hard work. And this is what we have in the Crossway Bible study series *Knowing the Bible*. The skilled authors and notable editors provide the contours of each book of the Bible as well as the grand theological themes that bind them together as one Book. Here, in a 12-week format, are carefully wrought studies that will ignite the mind and the heart."

R. KENT HUGHES, Visiting Professor of Practical Theology, Westminster Theological Seminary

"*Knowing the Bible* brings together a gifted team of Bible teachers to produce a high-quality series of study guides. The coordinated focus of these materials is unique: biblical content, provocative questions, systematic theology, practical application, and the gospel story of God's grace presented all the way through Scripture."

PHILIP G. RYKEN, President, Wheaton College

"These *Knowing the Bible* volumes provide a significant and very welcome variation on the general run of inductive Bible studies. This series provides substantial instruction, as well as teaching through the very questions that are asked. *Knowing the Bible* then goes even further by showing how any given text links with the gospel, the whole Bible, and the formation of theology. I heartily endorse this orientation of individual books to the whole Bible and the gospel, and I applaud the demonstration that sound theology was not something invented later by Christians, but is right there in the pages of Scripture."

GRAEME L. GOLDSWORTHY, former lecturer, Moore Theological College; author, *According to Plan*, *Gospel and Kingdom*, *The Gospel in Revelation*, and *Gospel and Wisdom*

"What a gift to earnest, Bible-loving, Bible-searching believers! The organization and structure of the Bible study format presented through the *Knowing the Bible* series is so well conceived. Students of the Word are led to understand the content of passages through perceptive, guided questions, and they are given rich insights and application all along the way in the brief but illuminating sections that conclude each study. What potential growth in depth and breadth of understanding these studies offer! One can only pray that vast numbers of believers will discover more of God and the beauty of his Word through these rich studies."

BRUCE A. WARE, Professor of Christian Theology, The Southern Baptist Theological Seminary

KNOWING THE BIBLE

J. I. Packer, Theological Editor
Dane C. Ortlund, Series Editor
Lane T. Dennis, Executive Editor

●　　●　　●　　●　　●　　●

Genesis	Psalms	Jonah, Micah, and Nahum	Ephesians
Exodus	Proverbs		Philippians
Leviticus	Ecclesiastes	Haggai, Zechariah, and Malachi	Colossians and Philemon
Numbers	Song of Solomon		
Deuteronomy	Isaiah	Matthew	1–2 Thessalonians
Joshua	Jeremiah	Mark	1–2 Timothy and Titus
Judges	Lamentations, Habakkuk, and Zephaniah	Luke	
Ruth and Esther		John	Hebrews
1–2 Samuel		Acts	James
1–2 Kings	Ezekiel	Romans	1–2 Peter and Jude
1–2 Chronicles	Daniel	1 Corinthians	1–3 John
Ezra and Nehemiah	Hosea	2 Corinthians	Revelation
Job	Joel, Amos, and Obadiah	Galatians	

●　　●　　●　　●　　●　　●

J. I. PACKER was the former Board of Governors' Professor of Theology at Regent College (Vancouver, BC). Dr. Packer earned his DPhil at the University of Oxford. He is known and loved worldwide as the author of the best-selling book *Knowing God*, as well as many other titles on theology and the Christian life. He served as the General Editor of the ESV Bible and as the Theological Editor for the *ESV Study Bible*.

LANE T. DENNIS is CEO of Crossway, a not-for-profit publishing ministry. Dr. Dennis earned his PhD from Northwestern University. He is Chair of the ESV Bible Translation Oversight Committee and Executive Editor of the *ESV Study Bible*.

DANE C. ORTLUND (PhD, Wheaton College) serves as senior pastor of Naperville Presbyterian Church in Naperville, Illinois. He is an editor for the Knowing the Bible series and the Short Studies in Biblical Theology series, and is the author of several books, including *Gentle and Lowly: The Heart of Christ for Sinners and Sufferers*.

2 CORINTHIANS

A 12-WEEK STUDY

Dane C. Ortlund

CROSSWAY®

WHEATON, ILLINOIS

Crossway is a publishing ministry of Good News Publishers.

VP		31	30	29	28	27	26	25	24	23	22
14	13	12	11	10	9	8	7	6	5	4	3

TABLE OF CONTENTS

SERIES PREFACE

KNOWING THE BIBLE, as the series title indicates, was created to help readers know and understand the meaning, the message, and the God of the Bible. Each volume in the series consists of 12 units that progressively take the reader through a clear, concise study of that book of the Bible. In this way, any given volume can fruitfully be used in a 12-week format either in group study, such as in a church-based context, or in individual study. Of course, these 12 studies could be completed in fewer or more than 12 weeks, as convenient, depending on the context in which they are used.

Each study unit gives an overview of the text at hand before digging into it with a series of questions for reflection or discussion. The unit then concludes by highlighting the gospel of grace in each passage ("Gospel Glimpses"), identifying whole-Bible themes that occur in the passage ("Whole-Bible Connections"), and pinpointing Christian doctrines that are affirmed in the passage ("Theological Soundings").

The final component to each unit is a section for reflecting on personal and practical implications from the passage at hand. The layout provides space for recording responses to the questions proposed, and we think readers need to do this to get the full benefit of the exercise. The series also includes definitions of key words. These definitions are indicated by a note number in the text and are found at the end of each chapter.

Lastly, for help in understanding the Bible in this deeper way, we would urge the reader to use the ESV Bible and the *ESV Study Bible*, which are available online at www.esvbible.org. The *Knowing the Bible* series is also available online.

May the Lord greatly bless your study as you seek to know him through knowing his Word.

J. I. Packer
Lane T. Dennis

WEEK 1: OVERVIEW

Getting Acquainted

"When I am weak, then I am strong," says Paul the apostle[1] (2 Cor. 12:10). This is the high point of 2 Corinthians, Paul's final letter to the church at Corinth. It is also the pervasive theme of the letter. God turns upside down our intuitive expectations of how the world works.

Throughout this letter Paul upends the natural Corinthian outlook on life, which is simply the natural universal outlook on life—that the way to joy and comfort and satisfaction is to put oneself forward, be impressive, throw one's weight around, exercise power and authority, have one's needs met. Paul confronts this deeply embedded natural outlook with a theology of the cross, in which serving the needs of others, even at great pain to ourselves, is the path to joy. Just as Jesus taught that a grain of wheat must fall to the ground and die before it bears fruit (John 12:24–25), so this paradoxical truth is the pervasive and unifying theme of 2 Corinthians—a theme rooted in Jesus' own experience of life through death and strength through weakness (2 Cor. 13:4).

This letter confronts each of us with the logic of the gospel, a logic that defies our natural inbred intuitions about the way to be happy. In our weakness, we discover the surprising power of God. (For further background, see the *ESV Study Bible*, pages 2219–2222; available online at esv.org.)

Placing It in the Larger Story

Jesus Christ has come in the flesh at the climax of human history. Paul the apostle has been chosen by the Lord to be a key player in proclaiming Christ

7

and his gospel to the world. After planting churches around the Mediterranean world, Paul writes letters back to these churches to strengthen them in their discipleship. The church at Corinth was particularly troubled, being tempted by false apostles to believe that Paul's weakness and sufferings proved he was a fake. Paul reminds the Corinthians of what has been true throughout redemptive history:[2] it is regularly the weak, the outsider, the crucified, through whom God powerfully works in the world.

Key Verse

"He said to me, 'My grace is sufficient for you, for my power is made perfect in weakness.' Therefore I will boast all the more gladly of my weaknesses, so that the power of Christ may rest upon me." (2 Cor. 12:9)

Date and Historical Background

As he wrote 2 Corinthians in AD 55/56, Paul had visited Corinth in recent months in what he describes in this letter as a "painful visit" (2 Cor. 2:1). Apparently, the Corinthian church had been largely hostile and demeaning toward Paul due to his general unimpressiveness in appearance and speech. Paul decided to give the church some space, so instead of an immediate visit he wrote them an anguished and tearful letter (2:3–4), which was then brought to them by Titus. This letter, written after 1 Corinthians but before 2 Corinthians, is now lost.

Titus reported back to Paul that much of the Corinthian church did indeed repent and again embrace Paul's authority (2 Cor. 7:5–16), though the sharp words throughout 2 Corinthians indicate there was a vocal minority still rejecting Paul. Perhaps Paul also feared that this minority would influence others in the church to join them against Paul.

All this explains the contorted nature of Paul's tone throughout 2 Corinthians— at times comforting his readers like a tender father, while at other times stringently attacking his accusers and defending his apostolic authenticity. Paul loves the Corinthians and wants them to see the power and glory of a gospel that humbles the powerful while strengthening the weak.

Outline

I. Paul's Defense of His Legitimacy as an Apostle (1:1–7:16)

  A. Salutation (1:1–2)

  B. Introduction (1:3–11)

  C. Paul's boast (1:12–2:17)

1. Content of Paul's boast (1:12–14)
2. Reason for Paul's first change of plans (1:15–22)
3. Reason for Paul's second change of plans (1:23–2:4)
4. Application of Paul's example to the Corinthians (2:5–11)
5. Paul's visit to Troas and Macedonia (2:12–17)

D. Paul's ministry of the new covenant as a ministry of the Spirit (3:1–18)

1. Reality of the Spirit in Paul's ministry (3:1–6)
2. Paul's interpretation of Exodus 32–34 (3:7–11)
3. Paul's application of Exodus 32–34 to his own situation (3:12–18)

E. Paul's encouragement in his ministry (4:1–6:13)

1. New covenant dawning of the new creation (4:1–6)
2. New covenant power of the resurrection (4:7–18)
3. New covenant motivation for the life of faith (5:1–10)
4. New covenant ministry of reconciliation (5:11–6:2)
5. New covenant support for the legitimacy of Paul's ministry (6:3–13)

F. Paul's call for church discipline as an expression of repentance (6:14–7:1)

G. Paul's joy over the repentant Corinthians (7:2–16)

II. Paul's Appeal to the Repentant Church in Corinth Regarding the Collection (8:1–9:15)

A. Collection as the grace of God (8:1–15)

B. Commendation of Titus and the brothers (8:16–9:5)

C. Generosity, joy, and the glory of God (9:6–15)

III. Paul's Appeal to the Rebellious Minority in Corinth (10:1–13:10)

A. Paul's defense of his humility as an apostle (10:1–11)

B. Paul's defense of his authority as an apostle (10:12–18)

C. Paul's defense of his boasting like a fool (11:1–21a)

D. Paul's boast in his service and suffering (11:21b–33)

E. Paul's boast in his heavenly vision and subsequent weakness (12:1–13)

F. Paul's final defense and appeal to the rebellious (12:14–13:10)

IV. Closing Greetings (13:11–14)

As You Get Started

Do you have a sense at the outset of this study of any specific emphases of 2 Corinthians? Without using your Bible, do any particular passages from

2 Corinthians come to mind? Has this letter already been meaningful to your own walk with the Lord in any specific ways?

What is your current understanding of what 2 Corinthians contributes to Christian theology? That is, how does this letter clarify your understanding of God, Jesus Christ, sin, salvation, the end times, or other doctrines?

What aspects of the epistle[3] of 2 Corinthians have confused you? Are there any specific questions you hope to have answered through this study?

As You Finish This Unit . . .

Take a few minutes to ask God to bless you with increased understanding and a transformed heart and life as you begin this study of 2 Corinthians.

Definitions

[1] **Apostle** – Means "one who is sent" and refers to one who is an official representative of another. In the NT, refers specifically to those whom Jesus chose to represent him.

[2] **Redemptive history** – A view of human history that observes the way God has graciously steered events and entered into our space and time repeatedly down through the centuries, culminating in the coming of Jesus Christ.

[3] **Epistle** – Basically the same as "letter." A literary form common in NT times. Epistles typically included: (1) statement of author and recipient; (2) brief greetings and expressions of thanks; (3) the body of the letter; (4) personal greetings and signature; and (5) a closing doxology or blessing. Twenty-one books of the NT are epistles.

WEEK 2: THE STRANGE PATH OF COMFORT

2 Corinthians 1:1–11

The Place of the Passage

Paul opens his letter by introducing himself as an apostle and then immediately teaching the Corinthians about the nature of true comfort. Unlike every other Pauline letter, Paul begins not by addressing the readers directly (usually with thanksgiving) but by speaking about God. Right from the start of this letter, Paul draws the Corinthians' eyes to the source of true comfort: God himself. And this comfort is experienced most profoundly in the midst of our own perplexities and trials.

The Big Picture

Second Corinthians 1:1–11 drives home the paradoxical nature of true comfort—those in Christ experience comfort not by avoiding but by *going through* affliction.

> **Reflection and Discussion**

Read through the complete passage for this study, 2 Corinthians 1:1–11. Then review the questions below concerning this introductory section to 2 Corinthians and write your notes on them. (For further background, see the *ESV Study Bible*, pages 2223–2224; available online at esv.org.)

1. Greeting (1:1–2)

Paul opens his letter by immediately designating himself as an apostle, literally "one who is sent." Skim through 2 Corinthians and note places where Paul returns to the theme of his legitimacy as a true apostle. What appears to have been the problem Paul is addressing regarding his own apostleship?

What does it mean for Paul to call the Christians of Achaia (the region in which Corinth was located) "saints" (1:1)? Are you a saint? Why or why not?

"Grace[1] to you and peace" (v. 2). With the exception of Galatians, Paul begins all his letters this way. Notice the wordplay used here, as explained in the *ESV Study Bible* notes. Why is grace the note on which Paul begins his letters? What does this remind us about concerning the Christian faith?

2. Comfort through Affliction (1:3–11)

Reflect on Paul's description of God the Father in verse 3. Consider your own life from this past week or so. Has God (as described in this verse) been real to you? Consider the calm that would descend into our generally frenetic lives if we were to walk with such a God and know him as such. Jot down a few thoughts for future reflection.

The Bible is not naive but utterly realistic. Notice this passage's honesty about the difficulties of life. According to verses 4 and 6, *why* do we experience affliction?

What does it mean to "share . . . in Christ's sufferings" (v. 5)? Does it mean Christ's sufferings were not enough to atone for our sin, so we need to help with our own suffering? Along with the *ESV Study Bible* note on this verse, consider also Philippians 3:8–11.

How would you put the message of 2 Corinthians 1:3–7 in your own words? Is this a familiar way to think about Christian discipleship in your own life and mind?

We can't be certain of the exact circumstances Paul is describing in verse 8, but we don't need to know exactly what he is referring to. The point is the purpose and result of this terrible experience. What, according to verse 9, is that purpose and result? What "death"-like experiences have you experienced in your past, or might you experience in your future, that make this verse a solid rock of hope and comfort?

How does Paul integrate Christian prayer into his delivery from death (v. 11)?

Read through the following three sections on *Gospel Glimpses*, *Whole-Bible Connections*, and *Theological Soundings*. Then take time to consider the *Personal Implications* these sections may have for you.

Gospel Glimpses

GRACE AND PEACE. This is the note on which the letter opens. The point of Christianity, according to Paul, is not to tell us to try harder or dig deeper or get more radical or obey better. There is a place for such exhortations. But the point, above all else, is to bring a word of comfort to the destitute, a word of grace to the sinful, a word of peace to the hostile. If the gospel has only one thing to say, this is it: *grace to you*. Be calmed. Be at rest. In Christ, the friend of sinners, there is grace for you.

COMFORT IN CHRIST. In fortifying the Corinthians through all their afflictions, Paul speaks of the comfort "we ourselves" have received from God

(2 Cor. 1:4) and experience through Christ (v. 5). The gospel has a clear, objective, black-and-white side to it, in which sinners are pardoned once and for all. But the gospel has also a subjective, felt side to it: *comfort*. In Christ, not only are we forgiven; we are comforted. The miseries of this fallen world, horrific or unbearable as they often are, can be borne, for we walk with Christ, the Savior sent from the God of all comfort. Making this happen is the ministry of the Holy Spirit,[2] who now dwells within believers (see also John 14:25–27).

▶ Whole-Bible Connections

AFFLICTION. In Eden, God and his people dwelt in happy fellowship. Sin had not come. Affliction was nonexistent. With the fall into sin, affliction and suffering began their long and sad history in this world. And God's own people are not immune to them. The book of Exodus, for example, shows the unique afflictions God's people often have. While not all affliction is a direct result of specific sins, sin in general is indeed the reason there is affliction in the world. The ultimate affliction is hell—which, for believers, Christ has borne in their place. One day, therefore, we will live in a new heaven and a new earth (Rev. 21:1), where no affliction will ever touch us. In the meantime, it is often through affliction that we are brought into true and close dependence on Christ.

▶ Theological Soundings

GOD'S FATHERHOOD. Paul speaks of the "God and Father of our Lord Jesus Christ" (2 Cor. 1:3). Christian orthodoxy teaches that Christ is the eternal Son of the Father. The Son was never created (contrary to what Arius and his followers taught in the early centuries of the church). Father and Son have existed in eternal, perfect fellowship. The marvel of history is that this Son took on flesh and entered into this fallen world so that we, too, could call God "Father," being adopted into God's family through the atoning work of Christ on our behalf. This is why Paul can call God "our Father" in verse 2 and the "Father of our Lord Jesus Christ" in verse 3.

UNION WITH CHRIST. Paul speaks of sharing in Christ's sufferings in verse 5. What does this mean? We can make sense of what Paul is saying only if we understand that Christians not only trust in Christ but are vitally united to him by the Holy Spirit. Paul explains this more fully elsewhere, where he speaks of sharing not only in Christ's sufferings but also in his death and resurrection (e.g., Rom. 6:1–6; Phil. 3:10–11). More fundamental to a Christian's identity than any other aspect of salvation is our union with Christ.

Personal Implications

Take time to reflect on the implications of 2 Corinthians 1:1–11 for your own life today. Consider what you have learned that might lead you to praise God, repent of sin, and trust in his gracious promises. Make notes below on the personal implications for your walk with the Lord of the (1) *Gospel Glimpses*, (2) *Whole-Bible Connections*, (3) *Theological Soundings*, and (4) this passage as a whole.

1. Gospel Glimpses

2. Whole-Bible Connections

3. Theological Soundings

4. 2 Corinthians 1:1–11

> ## As You Finish This Unit . . .

Take a moment now to ask for the Lord's blessing and help as you continue in this study of 2 Corinthians. And take a moment also to look back through this unit of study, to reflect on some key things that the Lord may be teaching you.

Definitions

[1] **Grace** – Unmerited favor, especially the free gift of salvation that God gives to believers through faith in Jesus Christ.

[2] **Holy Spirit** – One of the persons of the Trinity,[3] and thus fully God. The Bible mentions several roles of the Holy Spirit, including convicting people of sin, bringing them to conversion, indwelling them and empowering them to live in righteousness and faithfulness, supporting them in times of trial, and enabling them to understand the Scriptures. The Holy Spirit inspired the writers of Scripture, guiding them to record the very words of God. The Holy Spirit was especially active in Jesus' life and ministry on earth (e.g., Luke 3:22).

[3] **Trinity** – The Godhead as it exists in three distinct persons: Father, Son, and Holy Spirit. There is one God, yet he is three persons; there are not three Gods, nor do the three persons merely represent different aspects or modes of a single God. While the term Trinity is not found in the Bible, the concept is repeatedly assumed and affirmed by the writers of Scripture (e.g., Matt. 28:19; Luke 1:35; 3:22; Gal. 4:6; 2 Thess. 2:13–14; Heb. 10:29).

WEEK 3: PAUL'S PASTORAL STRATEGY

2 Corinthians 1:12–2:17

▲

The Place of the Passage

After opening with a powerful reminder of the comfort of the gospel (2 Cor. 1:1–11), Paul moves into the main body of the letter. In the second half of chapter 1 and all of chapter 2 Paul explains why he changed his mind and did not visit Corinth. Ultimately, Paul defends his actions as having been done out of love and in the best interests of the Corinthians. Here and throughout 2 Corinthians we see the deeply pastoral side of this letter.

The Big Picture

In 2 Corinthians 1:12–2:17 Paul explains why he had not visited the Corinthians as originally planned.

> ## Reflection and Discussion

Read through the entire text for this study, 2 Corinthians 1:12–2:17. Then interact with the following questions concerning this section of 2 Corinthians and record your notes on them. (For further background, see the *ESV Study Bible*, pages 2224–2226; available online at esv.org.)

Paul describes his "boast" in 2 Corinthians 1:12 and 14 and speaks of boasting in 2 Corinthians more often than in any of his other letters. Yet in 1 Corinthians 13:4 he had told the Corinthians that love does not boast. Evidently, there are bad and good kinds of boasting. How would you articulate the difference? Consider 1 Corinthians 1:31 and Galatians 6:14 as you answer.

What does Paul mean by the "day of our Lord Jesus" (2 Cor. 1:14)? In light of the Old Testament's theme of the "day of the LORD,"[1] what is Paul implicitly affirming about Christ?

What does verse 15 tell us about Paul's motives driving his travel plans? What does he ultimately want for the Corinthians? Note also verses 23–24.

Paul had apparently been accused of "vacillating" by not visiting Corinth (v. 17). How does Paul defend himself in verses 17–22? List several ways.

The first sentence of verse 20 is one of the richest statements of biblical theology[2] in all the Bible. What is Paul saying? How would you explain the role of Jesus as he relates to the entire Bible?

In verse 22 Paul calls the Holy Spirit our "guarantee" (note also 5:5; Eph. 1:14). This word means "down payment" or "deposit." Think of a down payment made on a house. What does that down payment indicate? What is Paul telling us about the role of the Holy Spirit?

In 2 Corinthians 2:1–4 Paul reiterates his love for the Corinthians and his desire for their welfare, mentioning the previous letter he had written to them (which we do not have). What does Paul say were his reasons for writing them that painful letter?

In 2:5–11 Paul calls the Corinthians to forgive and welcome a member of the church who had grievously sinned. Perhaps this member was the leader of the rebellion against Paul. Yet in 1 Corinthians 5 Paul had instructed this same church to expel a sinful man from the church—to hand him over to Satan and have nothing to do with him. What is the difference between these two situations?

What is the fundamental motivation for Christians to forgive others? Consider Matthew 6:14–15 and Colossians 3:13 as you answer.

Why was Paul's "spirit . . . not at rest" in Troas (2 Cor. 2:12–13)?

On the outside, Paul was anything but impressive. He was an afflicted, often rejected apostle. But in this final paragraph of chapter 2, Paul describes himself in terms of triumph and glory. What is Paul getting at? Note the chart on page 2225 of the ESV Study Bible listing "The Believer's Apparent (Temporal) Defeat" and "The Believer's Actual (Spiritual) Victory." How does this encourage you in your own walk with the Lord?

Read through the following three sections on *Gospel Glimpses, Whole-Bible Connections,* and *Theological Soundings.* Then take time to consider the *Personal Implications* these sections may have for you.

Gospel Glimpses

DIVINE ANOINTING. Paul writes that it is "God who establishes us with you in Christ, and has anointed us" (1:21). Throughout the Old Testament, anointing was how a man was marked out to be king. Over time the hope arose that one day God would provide a king, an anointed one, who would be the true and final king—the Hebrew word "Messiah" means "anointed one" (as does the Greek equivalent, "Christ"). Jesus is the Messiah, the anointed one, the true and final king. And—remarkably—Paul tells us here that we too, as those "in Christ," are anointed. This does not threaten Christ's own unique kingship, but it does mean that we are, as Paul says elsewhere, "fellow heirs with Christ" (Rom. 8:17). We who are united to Christ stand to inherit the entire cosmos—"All things are yours" (1 Cor. 3:21). We have been anointed. We are royalty. Unimaginably, but truly, we will rule the world, with Christ, one day soon.

FORGIVENESS. Paul calls the Corinthians to forgive the penitent sinner so that he is not overwhelmed with sadness (2 Cor. 2:7). We who believe in Christ have acknowledged that we too are sinners in need of forgiveness. When wronged by others, our only recourse in overcoming inevitable interpersonal bitterness and hardening is reflection on the forgiveness we ourselves have been offered in Christ (see also Matt. 18:21–35). Forgiveness is not sheer summoning of willpower. It is passing on horizontally what we have been given vertically.

Whole-Bible Connections

ALL THE PROMISES FULFILLED IN CHRIST. "All the promises of God find their Yes in him" (2 Cor. 1:20). What a strange statement! What does it mean for God's promises to "find their Yes" in Christ? Reading this statement in light of the entire New Testament teaching, we know that Paul is saying that the entire Old Testament, the whole history of God's dealings with his people and all that he has promised them, is fulfilled in and through Jesus. He clinches, integrates, brings to completion God's promises to be with his people, restore them, raise them from the dead, give them new life, and ultimately establish a new heaven and a new earth (Rev. 21:1). With Jesus, we see God as unshakably reliable, unswervingly trustworthy. Everything will be put right one day. Every longing of ours will be abundantly satisfied. For Christ has come. He is the living proof that God's words of promise and comfort are not empty statements.

Theological Soundings

THE HOLY SPIRIT. The Holy Spirit is our "guarantee" (1:22). This is a theologically rich word describing the Spirit as a pledge or "earnest"—a "first installment" of our salvation. This is a statement of inaugurated eschatology;[3] the Spirit is the sign that the new age has dawned. In the age between the first and second comings of Christ, the Holy Spirit is given to believers as proof they have been irreversibly swept up into this new age. In the present, life in this new age is marked by suffering and affliction. But there is a hidden glory in believers that will one day be fully manifest. The Holy Spirit, in the meantime, keeps, calms, animates, comforts, and helps us.

CHURCH DISCIPLINE. In 2:5–11 Paul calls for the restoration of a sinner. The church is called to discipline sinners, but care must be taken to understand why. The church is full of sinners, of course, and exists to welcome with open arms weak, faltering, sinful men and women. Church discipline is exercised toward *impenitent* sinners who profess to be Christians. We can put it like this: when a sinner is penitent (as here), pastors are called to protect the sinner from the church; when a sinner is impenitent (as in 1 Corinthians 5), pastors are called to protect the church from the sinner. All is done for the sake of the body.

Personal Implications

Take time to reflect on the implications of 2 Corinthians 1:12–2:17 for your own life today. Consider what you have learned that might lead you to praise God, repent of sin, and trust in his gracious promises. Make notes below on the personal implications for your walk with the Lord of the (1) *Gospel Glimpses*, (2) *Whole-Bible Connections*, (3) *Theological Soundings*, and (4) this passage as a whole.

1. Gospel Glimpses

2. Whole-Bible Connections

3. Theological Soundings

4. 2 Corinthians 1:12–2:17

> ## As You Finish This Unit . . .

Take a moment now to ask for the Lord's blessing and help as you continue in this study of 2 Corinthians. And take a moment to look back through this unit of study, to reflect on key things that the Lord may be teaching you.

Definitions

[1] **Day of the Lord** – According to the Old Testament prophets, God would come at the end of history, judging his enemies and restoring his people. This was referred to throughout the Old Testament as the "day of the LORD" (e.g., Isa. 13:9; Joel 1–3; Zech. 12–14; Mal. 4:5). Any day on which God took action in judgment might be called a "day of the LORD" (e.g., Amos 5:15–20).

[2] **Biblical theology** – Complementary to systematic theology, biblical theology is the discipline of tracing themes throughout the Bible—themes that climax in Christ, thus displaying the unity of the Bible.

[3] **Inaugurated eschatology** – "Eschatology" refers to "last things" and generally refers to what will happen at the end of all things when Jesus comes a second time. But the New Testament teaches that with the first coming of Christ, the final age or latter days were launched. We are those "on whom the end of the ages has come" (1 Cor. 10:11). The "eschaton," the final age, has dawned in Jesus. This is what is also referred to as the "already/not yet" of biblical theology.

25

WEEK 4: THE NEW COVENANT

2 Corinthians 3:1–18

The Place of the Passage

Paul brings to a close his explanation of why he had not visited Corinth by remarking that, while no one is "sufficient" for apostolic ministry (2 Cor. 2:16), he is nevertheless "commissioned by God" (v. 17). Paul picks up and develops this theme in chapter 3, defending his sufficiency for ministry despite how unimpressive he may seem by the world's standards. Paul develops his argument through a sustained comparison of his own ministry with that of Moses, noting that although Moses' ministry was glorious, Paul's is even more glorious—for it is the ministry of the Spirit, the ministry of the new covenant.[1]

The Big Picture

In 2 Corinthians 3:1–18 Paul explains his work as the ministry of the new covenant, a ministry of life and Spirit much more glorious than the ministry of Moses.

> ## Reflection and Discussion

Read through the passage for this study, 2 Corinthians 3:1–18. Then review the questions below concerning the ministry of the new covenant and write your notes on them. (For further background, see the *ESV Study Bible*, pages 2226–2228; available online at esv.org.)

1. Sufficiency from God (3:1–6)

In ancient times, leaders were often validated through recommendation letters—much like the references we provide when applying to a school or for a job. Paul has no such letter, but he has something even better; what is it, according to verse 2? What does Paul mean?

Throughout 2 Corinthians 3 Paul is drawing heavily on the Old Testament as he validates his ministry. Familiarize yourself with the following texts: Exodus 24:12; 31:18; 32:15. What is Paul referring to by "tablets of stone" (2 Cor. 3:3)? In light of Ezekiel 11:19 and 36:26, what is Paul saying in 2 Corinthians 3:3?

What does Paul identify as the source of his confidence before God (v. 4)? How does verse 5 drive this home even deeper?

Paul refers to the "new covenant" in verse 6. Read Jeremiah 31:31–34. What are the marks of the new covenant, according to this Old Testament passage? How is Paul bringing this text to bear in 2 Corinthians 3?

What does Paul mean by "letter" (v. 6)? Verse 6 is not the only time Paul sets up a letter/Spirit distinction—see also Romans 2:29 and 7:6. In light of all three texts, what is the basic contrast Paul is drawing out?

2. Paul versus Moses (3:7–18)

As you study 2 Corinthians 3:7–18, familiarize yourself first with Exodus 32–34, especially 34:29–35. How do you see Paul bringing the Old Testament to bear on his line of thought?

Make a list of everything Paul says about Moses' ministry versus everything he says about his own ministry. How would you sum up those differences?

Does Paul say Moses' ministry *lacked* glory, or *had* it (2 Cor. 3:7–11)? There was nothing inherently wrong with the old covenant—the problem was with *people*. As Paul explains in Romans 7, the law is holy and good; it is when sinful humans come under the law that the problem emerges! How does the ministry of the new covenant deal with and overcome this problem?

In verses 12–18 Paul begins to apply his argument to the present experience of his readers. What is his basic point of application?

Verse 18 is perhaps the richest statement in all the Bible about the way believers grow—the doctrine of progressive sanctification.[2] Paul say that "we all" (as opposed to just Moses) "with unveiled face" (as opposed to Moses' veiled face), "beholding the glory of the Lord, are being transformed into the same image from one degree of glory to another." The Greek word for "transformed" here is used just one other time in the New Testament, in Romans 12:2 ("Be *transformed* by the renewal of your mind"), where once more a gradual process of change is in view. Reflect on how Paul teaches that we are changed—namely, by beholding the Lord, not by sheer willpower, four- or twelve-step programs, or mind-emptying meditation. What does it mean to behold the glory of the Lord? How does that actually happen?

Read through the following three sections on *Gospel Glimpses*, *Whole-Bible Connections*, and *Theological Soundings*. Then take time to consider the *Personal Implications* these sections may have for you.

Gospel Glimpses

SUFFICIENCY FROM GOD. It is deeply hard-wired into all of us to generate our own "okayness," our own sufficiency. We want to make it on our own. We don't want help—especially when it comes to how we are accepted before God. But "confidence . . . toward God" (2 Cor. 3:4) remains elusive as long as we cling to our inbred tendency toward self-sufficiency. As we are seeing throughout 2 Corinthians, it is through entrusting ourselves to the Lord in our weakness and frailty that true strength and life blossom. As counterintuitive and even death-like as it feels, our confidence comes not from within us but from outside us—from God, who in Christ has drawn near to sinners and now indwells them by his Spirit.

FREEDOM. "Where the Spirit of the Lord is, there is freedom" (3:17). Life apart from Christ may feel like freedom to unbelievers, but those who have tasted walking with him know this to be the only true freedom. Life lived independently from Christ is slavery—slavery to the flesh, to self, to misery. In Christ we are freed—freed from condemnation, from spiritual blindness, from guilt and shame. To those on the outside, discipleship to Christ looks like bondage, but those on the inside know that discipleship to Christ is the only way to become truly human, to experience restoration to our true selves.

Whole-Bible Connections

COVENANT. The story of the Bible is carried forward by the series of covenants God initiates with his people—from Noah to Abram to Moses; some would even say God lived in covenant relationship with Adam in the garden. God binds himself to his people in a relationship of love. The motto of the covenants is, "You shall be my people, and I will be your God" (e.g., Ex. 6:7; Jer. 24:7). In 2 Corinthians 3 Paul speaks of the "new covenant" (v. 6), which transcends all the previous covenants and ensures life for God's people. This new covenant was secured in the death of Christ (Matt. 26:28). All today who trust in Christ are assured that God will be their God, having bound himself to them in covenant relationship.

IMAGE OF GOD. Paul says that by the Spirit we are being transformed "into the same *image*" (2 Cor. 3:18)—the same image of Christ that was distorted at the fall. In Christ, under the new covenant, by the Spirit, the image of God is restored. In the beginning God made human beings in his own image (Gen. 1:28). This image includes the various ways humans reflect God himself— living as moral beings and in relationships of love, and with divinely mandated rule over the earth and other creatures. The fall into sin did not obliterate, but did mar, the image. In Christ this restoration decisively begins, and one day it will come to glorious completion.

Theological Soundings

ILLUMINATION. One benefit given by the Holy Spirit is illumination—having our eyes opened to understand spiritual truth. Illumination more specifically refers to having one's eyes opened to understand Scripture, but it can refer to being given new insight on anything regarding our relationship to God. We must understand that as fallen people we are all naturally born blind to God, hostile to him and not comprehending the depth of our depravity or the provisions of his grace. By the Holy Spirit, he opens our eyes to know and love him.

DIVINE GLORY. Throughout 2 Corinthians 3 we hear of "glory"—first the lesser glory of the Mosaic covenant and then the greater glory of the new covenant. In both cases the source of this glory is the "glory of the Lord" (v. 18), seen through a veil in the old covenant and in an unveiled way in the new. What is God's glory? It is the sum of all he is and its resulting beauty, magnificence, resplendence. Its opposite is that which is boring, drab, lifeless, blank. God made us to reflect and even share in his glory (Rom. 8:30; 2 Thess. 2:14), which is the doctrine of glorification.[3]

Personal Implications

Take time to reflect on the implications of 2 Corinthians 3:1–18 for your own life today. Consider what you have learned that might lead you to praise God, repent of sin, and trust in his gracious promises. Make notes below on the personal implications for your walk with the Lord of the (1) *Gospel Glimpses*, (2) *Whole-Bible Connections*, (3) *Theological Soundings*, and (4) this passage as a whole.

1. Gospel Glimpses

2. Whole-Bible Connections

3. Theological Soundings

4. 2 Corinthians 3:1–18

As You Finish This Unit . . .

Take a moment now to ask for the Lord's blessing and help as you continue in this study of 2 Corinthians. And take a moment also to look back through this unit of study, to reflect on some key things that the Lord may be teaching you.

Definitions   ·

[1] **Covenant** – A binding agreement between two parties, typically involving a formal statement of their relationship, a list of stipulations and obligations for both parties, a list of witnesses to the agreement, and a list of curses for unfaithfulness and blessings for faithfulness to the agreement. The OT is more properly understood as the old covenant, meaning the agreement established between God and his people prior to the coming of Jesus Christ and the establishment of the new covenant (NT).

[2] **Sanctification** – The process of being conformed to the image of Jesus Christ through the work of the Holy Spirit. This process begins immediately after regeneration and continues throughout a Christian's life.

[3] **Glorification** – The work of God in believers to bring them to the ultimate and perfect stage of salvation—Christlikeness—following his justification and sanctification of them (Rom. 8:29–30).

WEEK 5: LIFE THROUGH DEATH

2 Corinthians 4:1–18

The Place of the Passage

In one of the richest and most precious chapters in the Bible, Paul explains why he does not "lose heart" (2 Cor. 4:1, 16) in his ministry. He continues to speak in terms of the paradox of the Christian life—here specifically as "life through death." It is through our weakness and even our death-like experiences that God demonstrates his surpassing power and sufficiency (v. 7). All the glory therefore belongs to God (v. 15).

The Big Picture

In 2 Corinthians 4:1–18 we see that while those in Christ deteriorate outwardly, internally they are being renewed by the gospel.

Reflection and Discussion

Read through the complete passage for this study, 2 Corinthians 4:1–18. Then review the questions below concerning this chapter of 2 Corinthians and write your notes below. (For further background, see the *ESV Study Bible*, pages 2228–2229; available online at esv.org.)

In the opening verses of chapter 4 Paul returns to the sincerity and guileless-ness of his motives for ministry. What motives does Paul elsewhere say do not fuel his ministry? Consult 2 Corinthians 2:17 and Galatians 1:10. What would you say is his fundamental motive for ministry? Along with this passage, consult 2 Corinthians 5:15 as you consider your answer.

Note in 4:3 the way Paul picks up the language of "veiling" from the previous chapter. What does it mean for the gospel to be veiled? In verse 4, to what or whom does Paul attribute this veiling?

Note the parallel phrases concluding verses 4 and 6. Write out these phrases below, indicating which words from verse 4 are parallel to words in verse 6. Jot down a few observations that arise from these parallels.

To what ancient event is Paul contrasting Christian conversion[1] in verse 6?
Consider 5:17 as you reflect on the answer.

What is Paul getting at by saying that the gospel is a "treasure in jars of clay"
(4:7)? What is the paradox here? What, according to verse 7, is the *purpose* of
this paradox?

Note the four pairings in verses 8 and 9. Why, in light of the surrounding
verses, do you think Paul says none of the horrible experiences of this life can
finally overcome us?

One of the truths of the New Testament is that Jesus died in our place. Another
truth, taught here and in Romans 6, is that we join him in his death. He died
as our substitute[2] with respect to sin, but union in his death informs our
Christian life. Trace Paul's logic through 2 Corinthians 4:10–12. What is Paul
essentially communicating?

In verse 13 Paul quotes from Psalm 116:10. The apostles often quote an Old Testament text as a "tip of an iceberg," intending the reader to recall the whole context of that Old Testament text. Flip back to that psalm and notice what the rest of that psalm says, especially the rest of verse 10. How is this a particularly relevant text for Paul to cite in 2 Corinthians 4?

Reflect on verses 16–18. This passage is a rock of hope and comfort amid the stormy seas of this fallen life. How does this text strengthen you today? Ponder especially the words "beyond all comparison" (v. 17).

Read through the following three sections on *Gospel Glimpses*, *Whole-Bible Connections*, and *Theological Soundings*. Then take time to consider the *Personal Implications* these sections may have for you.

Gospel Glimpses

A NEW CREATION, BY GRACE. In 2 Corinthians 4:6 Paul compares Christian salvation to the creation of the universe in Genesis 1. Just as God spoke light into existence, so he speaks the light of the knowledge of Christ into our dark hearts. Salvation is utterly from above—it is only of the Lord. While the Lord uses various means of grace to bring the gospel home to sinners—a sermon, a tract, the Bible, a friend, a neighbor—it is the Lord himself who draws us to himself and who opens our eyes. We contribute no more to our salvation than the dark void contributed to the creation of light.

LIFE OUT OF DEATH. We are united to Christ when we are saved, and this union means not only that our sins are forgiven but also that we join him in his death and resurrection. Paul goes so far as to speak of "carrying in the body the death of Jesus" (2 Cor. 4:9). In this way, resurrection life quietly blossoms, "that the life of Jesus may also be manifested in our bodies" (v. 10). At the heart of Christianity is the teaching that life comes through death—first for Christ, then for the Christian united to Christ.

Whole-Bible Connections

LIGHT AND DARKNESS. The theme of darkness and light runs right through the Bible, from the dawning of primordial light in Genesis 1:3–4 to the luminous radiance of God himself and the Lamb in Revelation 21:23–24 and 22:5. Throughout the Bible, the light motif is not limited to natural light. It reflects much more, from the dawning of creation itself (Gen. 1:2–4) to Israel's island of light amid the Egyptian plague of darkness (Ex. 10:23) to the pillar of cloud and fire to light Israel's way in the wilderness (Ex. 13:21; Neh. 9:12, 19; Ps. 78:14) to the perpetually burning lamp for light in the tabernacle (Ex. 27:20; Lev. 24:2; Num. 4:16) to the correlation between light and Torah (Ps. 119:105, 130; Isa. 51:4) to the Jewish association of light and joy (Est. 8:16; Ps. 97:11; Jer. 25:10) to the prophetic appropriation of light and darkness as moral categories (Isa. 5:20; 51:4; 59:9; Hos. 6:5; Mic. 7:9) to the hope of a restored world order in terms of light (Isa. 9:2; 30:26; 58:8; 60:1, 19–20). This motif of light, moreover, is not abstract brightness but is deeply Personal—its true source is the radiant luminosity of the face of God himself (Num. 6:25–26; Ps. 4:6; 34:5; 80:3, 7, 19; 89:15; compare Ps. 27:1; Mic. 7:8) reflected on the face of his servants (Ex. 34:29–35; Prov. 4:18; Isa. 60:5; Dan. 10:8), and ultimately of his Son (Mark 9:3; 2 Cor. 4:4; Heb. 1:3; Rev. 1:16), who is the light of the world (John 8:12). Since the Son's coming, therefore, "The darkness is passing away and the true light is already shining" (1 John 2:8). Light is a whole-Bible motif, popping up in redemptive history at one crucial moment after another.

Theological Soundings

RESURRECTION. The same God who "raised the Lord Jesus will raise us also with Jesus" (2 Cor. 4:14). It is Greek teaching, not biblical teaching, that says our souls will one day fly off to heaven and leave our bodies behind for good. On the contrary, when God first made us, he made us as *physical* beings. And he called our physical nature *good*. There is nothing inherently wrong with having a body, even though our bodies, just like our minds and hearts, are diseased by sin. Our final state, in the new heaven and new earth, will be an embodied one—with bodies that will never wear down, get sick, break bones, or contract cancer. We will be the fully human creatures, invincible and radiant and joy-ous, that we were made to be. And note that Paul says we will be raised "with Jesus"—another reference to our union to Christ. It is in union with him that we are guaranteed eventual resurrection. Put differently, the risen Christ is the first example history has ever seen of the physical state of being that all believers will one day enjoy. He is the "firstfruits" (1 Cor. 15:20–23), the first instance of restored, glorified humanity. When you look at the risen Lord, you look at *your* future.

Personal Implications

Take time to reflect on the implications of 2 Corinthians 4:1–18 for your own life today. Consider what you have learned that might lead you to praise God, repent of sin, and trust in his gracious promises. Make notes below on the personal implications for your walk with the Lord of the (1) *Gospel Glimpses*, (2) *Whole-Bible Connections*, (3) *Theological Soundings*, and (4) this passage as a whole.

1. Gospel Glimpses

2. Whole-Bible Connections

3. Theological Soundings

4. 2 Corinthians 4:1–18

> ### As You Finish This Unit . . .

Take a moment now to ask for the Lord's blessing and help as you continue in this study of 2 Corinthians. And take a moment also to look back through this unit of study, to reflect on some key things that the Lord may be teaching you.

Definitions

[1] **Conversion** – The result of turning away from sin, accepting the truth of the gospel of Jesus Christ, and submitting to him. Conversion is the human activity mirroring the divine activity of regeneration (granting of new birth).

[2] **Substitute** – To speak of Christ as our "substitute" refers to the doctrine of "substitutionary atonement." This is a way of understanding the purpose of Jesus' death on the cross: Jesus offered himself to die as a substitute for all who were to become believers. He took upon himself the punishment they deserve and thereby reconciled them to God.

WEEK 6: RECONCILIATION WITH GOD

2 Corinthians 5:1–21

▲

Paul moves at this point in his letter to explain more carefully the exact message of his new covenant ministry. He begins by explaining why we need not lose heart when our bodies are dying—we have a new, indestructible body coming (2 Cor. 5:1–10). Paul then moves into the message of reconciliation that God has entrusted to him (vv. 11–21).

The Big Picture

In 2 Corinthians 5:1–21 Paul tells us of our future hope of physical resurrection and the present offer of reconciliation with God that secures this hope.

> ## Reflection and Discussion

Read through 2 Corinthians 5:1–21, the focus of this week's study. Following this, review the questions below concerning this section of 2 Corinthians and write your responses. (For further background, see the *ESV Study Bible*, pages 2229–2231; available online at esv.org.)

What does Paul mean by the "tent that is our earthly home" and a "building from God . . . eternal in the heavens" (5:1)? Why might Paul have used this analogy?

In biblical teaching, believers who die today exist in the intermediate state,[1] living as disembodied spirits in the presence of God in heaven. But this is not our final state. Our final, permanent state after Jesus returns to earth will be an embodied physical existence with invincible bodies (v. 1; see also 1 Cor. 15:35–56; Phil. 3:10–11, 20–21). How does Paul speak of the intermediate state in 2 Cor. 5:2–4 and verse 8? What does he consider to be the *best* state of existence?

In verse 5 Paul calls the Spirit our "guarantee." He used this same language in 1:22, and also in Ephesians 1:14. In the context of 2 Corinthians 5:1–10, what is the significance of the Spirit as our down payment or first installment? What is Paul saying?

What, practically speaking, does Paul see in verses 6–7 as the result of the promise of future resurrection?

What does it mean to "walk by faith, not by sight"? Consider the context here, and the whole letter of 2 Corinthians.

In 5:9–10 Paul speaks of pleasing God before he speaks of appearing before the judgment seat of Christ. Does this contradict his teaching on justification[2] by faith? How do the teachings on justification by faith and appearing before the judgment seat of Christ cohere?

List all the reasons Paul gives in verses 11–21 for sharing with others the gospel of reconciliation with God.

Verses 14–15 provide a succinct summary of what it means to live as a disciple of Christ. How would you put this in your own words? Does this description of the Christian life match the way you normally think of life in Christ?

In verse 17 Paul says, literally, "Therefore, if anyone in Christ, new creation." He seems to be saying that if you have been united to Christ, you are swept into the new creation that dawned with the first coming of Christ. Read Isaiah 43:18–19; 65:17–23; 66:22–23 and reflect on what Paul may have had in mind when he spoke of this new creation.

Reflect on the language of reconciliation in 2 Corinthians 5:18–20. In everyday speech, what do we mean by "reconciling" two people? What change does this bring? What is Paul saying God was doing in Christ?

Verse 21 is one of the Bible's clearest statements of substitutionary atonement. (See 1 Peter 3:18 for another.) Specifically, we see here the doctrine of *imputa-*

tion.[3] Reflecting on the *ESV Study Bible* note on this verse, how would you put the doctrine of imputation in your own words? What should it mean for you as you roll out of bed tomorrow morning into another day?

Read through the following three sections on *Gospel Glimpses*, *Whole-Bible Connections*, and *Theological Soundings*. Then take time to consider the *Personal Implications* these sections may have for you.

Gospel Glimpses

RECONCILIATION WITH GOD. "In Christ God was reconciling the world to himself" (2 Cor. 5:19). The atoning work of Christ is so rich and profound that the Bible describes it in many different ways. Justification is law-court language, sanctification is temple/sacrifice language, adoption is family language, and so on—and reconciliation is *friendship* language. Its opposite is alienation. As fallen sinners, we are alienated from God. But in Christ, God has drawn near and restored us relationally to friendship again with him. And note that the initiative was wholly God's. *He* reconciled us to himself. The relationship is restored. This is great grace.

THE GREAT EXCHANGE. The German reformer Martin Luther called imputation the "happy exchange," in which we bankrupt sinners receive Christ's perfect righteousness, and Christ the righteous one takes on our bankruptcy and is punished for it at the cross. This is what 2 Corinthians 5:21 is all about (see also Rom. 4:4–8; 5:19). Luther spoke of this in terms of marriage, comparing imputation to a rich man marrying a poor woman—he takes on her poverty and she benefits from his wealth. Crucial to Christian health is beginning each day standing on the solid rock of Christ's righteousness, which has been imputed to us irreversibly, and then moving forward in the happy assurance that we are clothed forever in his righteousness.

Whole-Bible Connections

NEW CREATION. At the beginning of all things, God created the heavens and the earth. And at the end of all things, God will restore this universe to a new heaven and a new earth, as we see in books such as Isaiah and Revelation. Indeed, from one perspective, this is the whole point of the Bible—to tell the story of the journey from creation to new creation. And how do we get from one to the other, given the awful reality of human sin and rebellion? The answer is *Christ*. If anyone is united to Christ, they are caught up into the *shalom* of the new creation (2 Cor. 5:17), which will one day be perfected once and for all when Jesus comes to earth a second time and rinses clean this fallen world. If you are in Christ, you are guaranteed eventual restoration to what you were always meant to be—glorious, radiant, joyous, whole.

TEMPLE. Paul uses the language of "tent" and "building" and "dwelling" to speak of our physical bodies and their eventual resurrection (vv. 1–2). In doing so he is tapping into the whole-Bible theme of the temple, which in the Old Testament began as a portable temple called the tabernacle. The tabernacle (referred to sometimes as a tent) and the temple were where God met with his people. When Christ came, the New Testament says he "tabernacled" among us ("dwelt"; John 1:14, using the same Greek root as here in 2 Corinthians 5). His physical body was where the presence of God dwelt, for he was the incarnate Son. In the new earth, our physical bodies, indwelt by the Holy Spirit, will similarly be the place where God's glory dwells—a truth that has already been inaugurated (2 Cor. 3:18).

Theological Soundings

HEAVEN. In this present age before the return of Christ, believers will experience three stages of existence. First, we experience an *embodied, fallen* state of being in this life. Upon death those in Christ go to heaven to be with God and experience a *disembodied, unfallen* state. But this is not the end. Third, upon Christ's return to earth to establish his new and glorious kingdom once and for all, believers will experience *embodied, unfallen* existence. This is what we were created for. Our final state—what one theologian calls "life after life after death"—is the best of all, and will be like Eden restored, although without any possibility of sin's entering in.

JUSTIFICATION. The reformers of the sixteenth century called the doctrine of justification the key to the health of the church. What is it? Justification is the act of God accounting sinners acquitted of all charges and positively righteous in his sight. We are justified by faith, not by contributing any good works or obedience, but simply by looking to Christ and his finished work on the cross, receiving that work as a gift (Rom. 4:4–5). This is a scandalous doctrine, at the heart of the gospel, but it is gloriously true and is the lifeblood of all godliness. Only in justification is a sinner's conscience calmed so that he or she can be assured of God's fatherly favor.

Personal Implications

Take time to reflect on the implications of 2 Corinthians 5:1–21 for your own life today. Consider what you have learned that might lead you to praise God, repent of sin, and trust in his gracious promises. Make notes below on the personal implications for your walk with the Lord of the (1) *Gospel Glimpses*, (2) *Whole-Bible Connections*, (3) *Theological Soundings*, and (4) this passage as a whole.

1. Gospel Glimpses

2. Whole-Bible Connections

3. Theological Soundings

4. 2 Corinthians 5:1–21

> ## As You Finish This Unit . . .

Take a moment now to ask for the Lord's blessing and help as you continue in this study of 2 Corinthians. And take a moment also to look back through this unit of study, to reflect on some key things that the Lord may be teaching you.

Definitions

[1] **Intermediate state** – The state of existence believers experience immediately after death and before resurrection. Most Protestant theologians believe that, after death, the souls of believers immediately enter God's presence, although they remain in disembodied form as they await the final resurrection, when they will be reunited with their bodies. See the *ESV Study Bible* note on 1 Corinthians 15:23.

[2] **Justification** – The act of God's grace in bringing sinners into a new covenant relationship with himself and counting them as righteous before him through the forgiveness of sins (Rom. 3:20–26).

[3] **Imputation** – Generally speaking, to impute is to attribute something to someone or credit it to his or her account. More specifically, imputation refers to God's crediting to every believer the righteousness of Jesus Christ; we guilty sinners receive Christ's perfect record, while he bears the punishment for our guilt on the cross. This imputation is an aspect of justification.

WEEK 7: TRUE RELATIONSHIPS AND TRUE REPENTANCE

2 Corinthians 6:1–7:16

▲

Paul moves now to demonstrate once more the sincerity and authenticity of his work as an apostle sent from God. The first half of chapter 6 is one of the many powerful depictions of God's power in Paul's weakness, and in the second half of the chapter Paul exhorts the true believers in Corinth not to join hands with those rejecting his apostolic ministry. In chapter 7 Paul continues arguing for his apostolic authority and distinguishes between true and false repentance[1]—suggesting that he prompted true, godly grief among the Corinthians, ultimately for their own good.

The Big Picture

Second Corinthians 6–7 demonstrates Paul's apostolic authority and his sincere desire for the Corinthians' good.

> ### Reflection and Discussion

Read through the complete passage for this study, 2 Corinthians 6:1–7:16. Then review the questions below concerning this transition section of 2 Corinthians and write your notes on them. (For further background, see the *ESV Study Bible*, pages 2231–2233; available online at esv.org.)

In 2 Corinthians 6:2 Paul quotes Isaiah 49:8. Scan the context of Isaiah 49 and consider what Paul is saying to the Corinthians. Paul goes on to say that the day of restoration promised in Isaiah 49 has dawned in the present time. Remembering what Paul has just said in 2 Corinthians 5:17, what is Paul's reason for quoting Isaiah 49:8?

Ponder the paradoxes of 2 Corinthians 6:3–10—utter realism about difficulties, yet supreme hopefulness as well. How does this list support Paul's ministry as an apostle? Consider especially verse 10 as you bridge this passage into your own heart and life. How does this verse affect you? Do you find it liberating?

Paul is sometimes viewed by Christians as a complicated, somewhat dry, deeply theological thinker. He was certainly a powerful mind. But notice 6:11 (as well as 7:2). What do you see of Paul here? What might we today learn from what Paul writes in this verse?

One of the great themes of the Bible is the need for God's people to separate themselves from the godless world around them. What Old Testament text(s) are cited here, and what basic point is Paul making in 6:14–7:1?

What is the motivation for personal holiness[2] in 7:1? Reflect on how this is a gospel motivation. Is Paul saying that we should be holy *so that* God will give us promises, or *because* God has already given us promises? What are the promises being referred to (see 6:16–18)?

What paradox do you see in 7:4, and how does this relate to the letter as a whole? Recall what we said in Week 1 of this study about strength through weakness as the macro-theme of the letter.

In 7:5 Paul picks up the narrative where he left off in 2:13. What has Paul been writing about in the five intervening chapters? Why do you suppose he spends so much time on this?

Paul reflects at length on the difference between "godly grief" and "worldly grief." How do these look the same on the outside? How are they different, according to this passage? Reflect for a moment on an instance of each in your own life.

What role does Titus play throughout this chapter? What do you take from this as you consider your own life and ministry in the local church?

Read through the following three sections on *Gospel Glimpses*, *Whole-Bible Connections*, and *Theological Soundings*. Then take time to consider the *Personal Implications* these sections may have for you.

Gospel Glimpses

SORROWFUL, YET ALWAYS REJOICING. Becoming a Christian does not exempt us from life's troubles. Indeed, there are certain troubles that are unique to being a Christian (Acts 14:22; 2 Tim. 3:12). But beneath all the trials of life lies a deeper reality: adoption into God's family, being indwelt by the Holy Spirit, safe and secure in the arms of God. Amid all the darkness of life, this gracious salvation and the multifaceted comfort it brings is our lifeline. The troubles of life bring us into deeper solidarity with Christ and deeper fellowship with him. This is why Paul can say he is "sorrowful, yet always rejoicing" (2 Cor. 6:10).

INDICATIVES, IMPERATIVES. Throughout the Bible the "indicatives" (what God has done for us) fuel the imperatives (how we respond in obedience to him). Our natural default mode is to think the imperatives drive the indicatives—that our obedience secures God's favor. But in the gospel it is God's favor, already won for us by Christ, that impels heartfelt obedience. In 2 Corinthians 7:1 we see this dynamic, as Paul exhorts the Corinthians to obedience based on God's promises rather than exhorting them to holiness as a way to secure God's promises: "Since we have these promises, beloved, let us cleanse ourselves from every defilement of body and spirit, bringing holiness to completion in the fear of God."

Whole-Bible Connections

INAUGURATED ESCHATOLOGY. Paul says that "now is the favorable time" and "now is the day of salvation" (2 Cor. 6:2). These statements are often taken as encouraging evangelistic activity—today is the day for you to be saved! While these texts do not mean less than this, they have something deeper and bigger to say. In 2 Corinthians 6:2, Paul is picking up on the quote he has just cited from Isaiah 49:8. In Isaiah we read of the coming day of salvation and judgment. Paul is saying that, in the first century, this final day has dawned—the future time Isaiah prophesied is now here! We call this "inaugurated eschatology"— that is, the last time (eschatology) has begun now (has been inaugurated). When Christ returns a second time, these final days will be consummated, or completed. We live now in the overlap of the ages—the new age has dawned, but the old age continues right alongside it. One day, when Christ returns, this old age will come to an end and the cosmos will be washed clean. Then the new age will be all we know. There will be no more tears or pain or anguish.

TEMPLE. Paul again draws attention to the temple theme, the "dwelling" place of God (2 Cor. 6:16). The entire story of the Bible is about regaining God's dwelling with humanity that was fractured in Eden. The tabernacle, then the temple, then Christ the true temple, and then the people of God as part of that temple as they are united to Christ—all this carries along this important whole-Bible theme. For more on this, see "Temple" under "Whole-Bible Connections" in Week 6 of this study.

Theological Soundings

GRACE. Paul appeals to the Corinthians "not to receive the grace of God in vain" (2 Cor. 6:1). God's grace is the most marvelous, scandalous reality in the universe—undeserved mercy pouring out of the heart of God onto and into sinners. But it must be *received*. To reject it is to squander it, to resist it, to say "No, thank you." If we appear to receive God's grace but then in time go back to our former lives, we abandon the grace of God and show that it never really took root within us. The grace of God is an active power (Rom. 1:16), training us for godliness (Titus 2:11–12).

SATAN. We are given further teaching in this passage on the figure of Satan, whom Paul here calls "Belial" (2 Cor. 6:15). This name comes from a Hebrew word meaning "worthlessness." Scripture identifies Satan from various angles as the accuser (Zech. 3:1), the tempter (Matt. 4:3), the deceiver (Rev. 12:9), and our enemy in other ways too. Here we are reminded that he is worthless, and that those who belong to Christ must have nothing to do with him. He and his agenda are not even to be flirted with, but avoided at all costs. Satan's purpose is misery and destruction. He is the father of worthlessness as a way of life.

Personal Implications

Take time to reflect on the implications of 2 Corinthians 6:1–7:16 for your own life today. Consider what you have learned that might lead you to praise God, repent of sin, and trust in his gracious promises. Make notes below on the personal implications for your walk with the Lord of the (1) *Gospel Glimpses*, (2) *Whole-Bible Connections*, (3) *Theological Soundings*, and (4) this passage as a whole.

1. Gospel Glimpses

2. Whole-Bible Connections

3. Theological Soundings

4. 2 Corinthians 6:1–7:16

> ## As You Finish This Unit . . .

Take a moment now to ask for the Lord's blessing and help as you continue in this study of 2 Corinthians. And take a moment also to look back through this unit of study, to reflect on some key things that the Lord may be teaching you.

Definitions

[1] **Repentance** – A complete change of heart and mind regarding one's overall attitude toward God or one's individual actions. True regeneration and conversion is always accompanied by repentance.

[2] **Holiness** – A quality possessed by something or someone set apart for a special role in relation to God. When applied to God himself, it refers to his utter perfection and complete transcendence over creation. God's people are called to imitate his holiness (Lev. 19:2), which means being set apart from sin and reserved for his purposes.

WEEK 8: WHERE REAL GENEROSITY COMES FROM

2 Corinthians 8:1–9:15

The Place of the Passage

Paul has now defended at length his true legitimacy as an apostle, against objections to the contrary from some at Corinth. He now encourages the Corinthians to join once more in collecting a financial gift for believers in Jerusalem (see 8:10–11). Throughout these two chapters we again see Paul appealing to the grace of God, and also once again relying heavily on his coworkers.

The Big Picture

In 2 Corinthians 8:1–9:15 Paul exhorts the Corinthians toward financial generosity in light of the gospel of grace.

> ## Reflection and Discussion

Read the entire text for this week's study, 2 Corinthians 8:1–9:15. Then review the following questions concerning this section of 2 Corinthians and write your notes on them. (For further background, see the *ESV Study Bible*, pages 2233–2235; available online at esv.org.)

Note what Paul says in describing the generosity of the Macedonians in the opening verses of 2 Corinthians 8. Most of the time we think of *grace* in terms of something the Macedonians themselves would have received. How can Paul here (and throughout these two chapters) call *their* generosity the "grace of God"? Describe in your own words the dynamics of the heart[1] taking place in the Macedonians.

Paul says his exhortation to the Corinthians to contribute is not a command (8:8). What, then, is it? What does it mean to respond to this type of leading as compared to obeying a command? What differentiates these two kinds of obedience?

Ponder verse 9, one of the richest statements of the gospel in the Bible. What is Paul saying? How is he connecting money and the gospel?

What principle is Paul laying down in 8:12? How does Jesus' teaching in Luke 21:1–4 complement Paul's words here?

Read the story (Ex. 16:9–21) Paul alludes to in 2 Corinthians 8:15. How is Paul bringing that story to bear on the point he is currently making? Remember that the theme of 2 Corinthians, as we are seeing, is that the ways of God are upside down from the ways of the world and our natural intuitions.

List the various motives Paul cites in the paragraph from 8:16 to 8:24. How would you summarize Paul's reasons for seeking financial relief for the Jerusalem believers?

What is Paul's strategy for motivating the Corinthians toward financial giving in 9:1–5? Note especially the language of "ready/readiness" in this paragraph.

Paul brings forward yet another motive for giving in 9:6. What is it? How do we see this principle at work in the natural world (note, e.g., Jesus' words in

John 12:24)? Is Paul saying the way to get rich is to give away money? If not, what *is* his point?

_____

_____

_____

_____

_____

According to 2 Corinthians 9:8, what is the ultimate source of our good works?

_____

_____

_____

_____

Paul concludes his two-chapter discourse on money on the same note with which he began: the grace of God (8:1; 9:14). Specifically, Paul speaks of God's "inexpressible gift" (9:15). What is he referring to? How is this an "inexpressible gift" and the supreme instance of God's grace? As you look back over 2 Corinthians 8–9, how does this inexpressible gift fuel generosity?

_____

_____

_____

_____

_____

Read through the following three sections on *Gospel Glimpses*, *Whole-Bible Connections*, and *Theological Soundings*. Then take time to consider the *Personal Implications* these sections may have for you.

Gospel Glimpses

OUR POVERTY FOR HIS RICHES. As in 2 Corinthians 5:21, Paul speaks of the "great exchange" in which Jesus switches places with guilty rebels so that we get his righteousness[2] and he takes our sins. But notice that Paul takes that great reality and transposes it into the realm of money, the topic at hand (8:9). We see Paul's resilient gospel-centeredness in this—whatever the subject, the gospel is never far from his mind. And indeed, he understands that the only true power to give cheerfully (9:7) is the gospel of grace, in which we spiritual paupers are granted inexhaustible riches. This is a grace worth singing over, a grace worthy of our all. "Thanks be to God for his inexpressible gift!" (9:15).

GRACE ABOUNDING. Note the piled-up superlatives of 9:8: "God is able to make *all* grace abound to you, so that having *all* sufficiency in *all* things at *all* times, you may abound in *every* good work." Paul uses the same Greek word five times to drive home the exhaustive grace of God and the abundant resource it is for believers. Are you running on empty? Do you feel dry or exhausted? Go to him. Jesus Christ is a fountain of living water, never running dry, never failing to strengthen and stabilize and support. Grace brought us into the kingdom, and grace will sustain us until we are with Christ in heaven.

Whole-Bible Connections

HELPING THE POOR. The poor believers in Jerusalem are Paul's concern throughout these two chapters of 2 Corinthians. Throughout the Pentateuch[3] God repeatedly exhorts his people to care for the poor among them. This becomes a resounding theme throughout these early chapters of the Bible (e.g., Ex. 22:25; 23:11; Lev. 14:21), especially Deuteronomy (e.g., Deut. 15:4–11; 24:12–15). It is then picked up frequently by the prophets later in the Old Testament (e.g., Isa. 58:7; Jer. 2:34; Amos 5:11). And in the New Testament it is clearly an important theme (e.g., Acts 6:1; James 1:26–2:7; 5:1–6). The Bible does not suggest that generosity to the poor is the fundamental human dilemma to be solved, as some advocates of social justice sometimes claim. The supreme need is grace for the soul, not money for the body. The supreme example of help to the poor is the Lord Jesus himself, who left the riches of heaven to take on the poverty of our own flesh, even going to death on a cross. This is the supreme message of the Bible: grace for spiritually poor sinners. But we must not so spiritualize the Bible's teaching that we neglect the important "grace" (as Paul calls it throughout 2 Corinthians) of tangible mercy to the poor.

Theological Soundings

OBEDIENCE. Throughout these two chapters of 2 Corinthians Paul is unashamedly calling on the Corinthians to give to the poor Christians in Jerusalem. Does this jeopardize the teaching that salvation is wholly by grace? Absolutely not! Instead, it is the very gospel of grace itself that motivates such obedience. Our obedience and God's grace are not related as cause and effect, as if our obedience causes God to be gracious to us. Then grace would not be grace. Rather, it is exactly the other way round—God's grace causes our obedience. Antinomianism teaches that God's grace negates the need for our obedience. Legalism teaches that obedience triggers God's grace. Both teachings are wrong. As we have seen throughout 2 Corinthians 8–9, God's grace is the fuel for our obedience.

GOD'S GLORY. Throughout these two chapters Paul speaks of the "glory of the Lord" (8:19) and his desire to "glorify God" (9:13). What is the glory of God? It is *his very God-ness.* Who he is. It is the sum of all his perfections, the total picture, his resplendence and magnificence, his beauty and loveliness. True Christians are those whose fundamental heart desires have been flipped inside out so that they no longer crave their own glory but the Lord's. To be sure, we slip back into little self-glory quests all the time as believers! But grace exists for this too. When this happens we laugh at our silliness, turn afresh to the Lord, and ask his forgiveness and help. We become truly human, who we were made to be, only when we are seeking to honor him.

Personal Implications

Take time to reflect on the implications of 2 Corinthians 8:1–9:15 for your own life today. Consider what you have learned that might lead you to praise God, repent of sin, and trust in his gracious promises. Make notes below on the personal implications for your walk with the Lord of the (1) *Gospel Glimpses*, (2) *Whole-Bible Connections*, (3) *Theological Soundings*, and (4) this passage as a whole.

1. Gospel Glimpses

2. Whole-Bible Connections

3. Theological Soundings

----

4. 2 Corinthians 8:1–9:15

▶ As You Finish This Unit . . .

Take a moment now to ask for the Lord's blessing and help as you continue in this study of 2 Corinthians. And take a moment also to look back through this unit of study, to reflect on some key things that the Lord may be teaching you.

Definitions

[1] **Heart** – In the Bible, the heart is the animating center of all that humans do and think.

[2] **Righteousness** – The quality of being morally right and without sin. One of God's distinctive attributes. God imputes or accounts righteousness to (justifies) those who trust in Jesus Christ.

[3] **Pentateuch** – The first five books of the Bible, also sometimes called the Law or Torah.

Week 9: True versus False Leadership

2 Corinthians 10:1–11:15

The Place of the Passage

Paul turns at this point in his letter and directly addresses those opposed to his ministry due to his alleged weakness. For this reason some have trouble believing this is the same man who had written in such a warm pastoral tone earlier in the letter! But it is the audience, not the author, that has shifted. Here Paul will defend his ministry by continuing to drive home the truths that God's ways are not our ways and that the gospel gives believers a paradigm upside down from that of the world. Under the gospel, and supremely for Christian leaders, weakness is strength and life comes through death.

The Big Picture

In 2 Corinthians 10:1–11:15 Paul teaches us that true leadership is outwardly unimpressive and is for others' good, as opposed to false leadership, which is outwardly impressive and self-serving.

> ## Reflection and Discussion

Read through the complete text for this study, 2 Corinthians 10:1–11:15. Then review the questions below concerning this passage of 2 Corinthians and write your notes on them. (For further background, see the *ESV Study Bible*, pages 2235–2237; available online at esv.org.)

What does it mean for Paul to appeal to the Corinthians "by the meekness and gentleness of Christ" (10:1)? Why might Paul have spoken of Christ in this way, given what was happening in the Corinthian church?

What are the weapons of divine warfare Paul refers to in 10:3–4? How does this differ from the "weapons" or tactics employed by his opponents in Corinth?

Paul does indeed "boast" of his authority. But to what end (10:8)? What is the purpose of this authority, unlike the motives of his opponents? See also 12:19 and 13:10 as you answer. Reflect on what Christ has done for us and how Paul's motive in ministry is a "gospel" motive.

Note what Paul's opponents are saying of him in 10:10. Reflect on the opening two chapters of 1 Corinthians, especially 1 Corinthians 2:1–5. How does Paul handle his opponents' attacks throughout the Corinthian correspondence? Do you find this principle personally liberating in your own life, given the inadequacies you feel?

In light of 2 Corinthians 10:12, how are Paul's opponents establishing their own credibility? What is Paul's alternative to this?

Read Romans 14:14–17. How do Paul's words there inform his line of reasoning in 2 Corinthians 10:15–16?

What does it mean to "boast in the Lord" (10:17)? How is this the polar opposite of the conduct of those opposing Paul?

Follow the analogy Paul uses in 11:1–3. Who, spiritually speaking, is the father, the daughter, the husband, and the one leading the daughter astray in this analogy? What light does this shed on how Paul views his relationship to the Corinthians?

How would it have been "humbling" to Paul to preach the gospel at no charge to the Corinthians (11:7)?

Consider Paul's description of the false leaders in 11:13. As you ponder 2 Corinthians 10:1–11:15, how would it have been evident that these men were false teachers?

Read through the following three sections on *Gospel Glimpses*, *Whole-Bible Connections*, and *Theological Soundings*. Then take time to consider the *Personal Implications* these sections may have for you.

Gospel Glimpses

THE GENTLENESS OF CHRIST. Paul appeals to the "meekness and gentleness of Christ" (2 Cor. 10:1). This is a striking appeal in light of how forcefully he must deal with the beguiling tactics of opponents undermining his ministry. But in this appeal he is drawing our minds to the very heart of Christ. The only time in all four Gospels where Jesus discusses his heart is in Matthew 11:29, where he says he is "gentle and lowly in heart." We know much about his teachings, his doctrine, his view of how he fulfilled the Old Testament, and so on. But only here does he tell us of his heart. And when he does, he identifies his heart as gentle, lowly, meek. This is who Christ is. He knows what it is to be angry (John 2:13–17). He can weep over the fallenness of this world (Matt. 23:37). But what is his *heart?* Paul captures it in 2 Corinthians 10:1: "meekness and gentleness."

BOASTING IN CHRIST. Throughout these chapters Paul does not eradicate all boasting whatsoever, instead channeling it in a gospel direction: boasting in Christ. The Christian does indeed boast. But our boast has been transferred from boasting in self, and all the misery that accompanies this, to boasting in Christ, and the freedom that accompanies this. In Christ we are freed from the exhausting need to locate our security in what we bring to the table—our own accomplishments, righteousness, performance, abilities. Our confidence now lies outside of us, in Christ. The pressure is off. We are free.

Whole-Bible Connections

ADAM AND EVE. Paul takes us back to the garden of Eden and the beginning of humanity (11:1–3). He reminds us that sin was introduced into the world through the deception of Adam and Eve. As the biblical story unravels, we learn that in Adam and Eve's fall the entire world was brought into ruin and under the sway of sin and Satan. Adam represented all of us; but for those who trust Christ, he becomes their new representative (Rom. 5:12–19). One day, in the new earth, this New Adam will reign in perfect justice and peace in a restored world. No more deception. No more sin and Satan. All will be put right. We will live forever as the bride of Christ, in "sincere and pure devotion" to him (11:3).

MARRIAGE. Paul speaks of the Corinthians' relationship to Christ, after they embraced the gospel when he first preached it to them, as a wedding day. Paul is the father who "betrothed" them "to one husband," Christ (11:2). Marriage is a divinely ordained institution reaching back to the very dawn of human history, as God gave Adam a wife, "a helper fit for him" (Gen. 2:18). This is a great blessing. But it is a pointer to the greatest blessing—God's great salvation in Christ, in which believers become the bride of Christ. God did not give us marriage randomly; he gave us marriage explicitly to show us the gospel and what it means for a sinner to be welcomed home to God, restored to his Creator (Eph. 5:32). At the end of history, when Christ comes a second time, the scene will be like a wedding day (Rev. 21:2). Marriage penetrates to the heart of the meaning of the universe—the love of a God too great to be contained within the Trinity, compelled to spill out and include humanity in its embrace.

Theological Soundings

SATAN. We learn here in 2 Corinthians 11 of a particular characteristic of Satan—he "disguises himself as an angel of light" (11:14). This helps us to understand why sin runs so rampant in the world today and in our own lives— it *looks* good. This is the essence of sin and Satan—ugliness masquerading as beauty. But it is a counterfeit. If Satan were naturally repelling, no one would be drawn to him or his realm.

FINAL JUDGMENT. "Their end will correspond to their deeds" (11:15). God is a God of justice. For him to wink at sin, to look the other way, is not kindness on his part; if he did that, he would cease being God. The natural reflex of his holy righteousness is to right what is wrong. This is who he is. This is part of what makes him holy and worthy of our worship. Much today is out of accord with justice, but the Bible is clear that one day all will be put right. The Lord of history will bring universal justice and judgment.[1] We see a glimpse of this in 2 Corinthians 11, as Paul tells the Corinthians that servants of Satan, while disguising themselves now as servants of what is right, will be judged appropriately and accordingly one day. This is a calming and hope-giving truth for believers today, especially for those who experience the hell of injustice at the hands of others.

Personal Implications

Take time to reflect on the implications of 2 Corinthians 10:1–11:15 for your own life today. Consider what you have learned that might lead you to praise God, repent of sin, and trust in his gracious promises. Make notes below on the personal implications for your walk with the Lord of the (1) *Gospel Glimpses*, (2) *Whole-Bible Connections*, (3) *Theological Soundings*, and (4) this passage as a whole.

1. Gospel Glimpses

2. Whole-Bible Connections

3. Theological Soundings

4. 2 Corinthians 10:1–11:15

As You Finish This Unit . . .

Take a moment now to ask for the Lord's blessing and help as you continue in this study of 2 Corinthians. And take a moment also to look back through this unit of study, to reflect on some key things that the Lord may be teaching you.

Definition

[1] **Judgment** – Any assessment of something or someone, especially moral assessment. The Bible also speaks of a final day of judgment when Christ returns, when all those who have refused to repent will be judged (Rev. 20:12–15).

Week 10: Strength through Weakness

2 Corinthians 11:16–12:10

▲

The Place of the Passage

After several chapters defending his ministry and showing how the gospel in various ways upends the world's mind-set regarding affliction, joy, grief, and money, Paul comes to the climax of his letter. Here at the heart of 2 Corinthians the apostle gives us the key that unlocks this entire letter and indeed his entire ministry: strength through weakness. It is in our unimpressiveness, our afflictions, our inadequacies, our pain, that God's power and grace are manifested. That is backward to the way we naturally think. This culmination of 2 Corinthians is a timely word to each generation of the church, including ours today.

The Big Picture

In 2 Corinthians 11:16–12:10, Paul crystallizes the principle fundamental to his apostolic ministry and to our Christian lives today: strength through weakness.

Reflection and Discussion

Read through the complete passage for this study, 2 Corinthians 11:16–12:10. Then review the questions below on this climactic section of 2 Corinthians and record your notes and reflections. (For further background, see the *ESV Study Bible*, pages 2237–2239; available online at esv.org.)

Why would Paul refer to himself as a fool throughout 11:16–21? What does he mean by this? What other ironies[1] do you see in these verses—in verse 21, for example?

As he did in 6:3–10, Paul mixes good and bad, blessings and pains, in the list of 11:22–29. Why would he do this?

Why would Paul have received 39 lashes? What kinds of breaches of the law would incur this punishment?

In 11:30 Paul concludes his litany of sufferings amid privileges and gives the reason for his boasting. What is that reason? What is Paul's strategy toward the Corinthians here?

Paul concludes chapter 11 by mentioning an experience in which he was ingloriously brought down. He then goes on in chapter 12 to describe an experience in which he was gloriously brought up. What was this glorious experience?

Why might Paul speak of himself in the third person in 12:2–4?

Why was a "thorn" given to Paul? Notice that the reason is given twice, at both the beginning and the end of verse 7. Yet Paul says that this thorn was from Satan.[2] Given the reason for the thorn, could it have been *ultimately* from Satan?

It is evidently not immature to ask the Lord to remove the "thorns" of our lives. But he may choose to allow our thorns to remain. If he does, what great reality will support us, according to 12:9? What was the result of this reality for Paul in 12:9–10?

"When I am weak, then I am strong" (12:10). Put that sentence into your own words. How have you seen this theme throughout 2 Corinthians (and also 1 Corinthians, if you are familiar with that letter)? Note the chart on page 2238 of the *ESV Study Bible* as you answer.

Read through the following three sections on *Gospel Glimpses*, *Whole-Bible Connections*, and *Theological Soundings*. Then take time to consider the *Personal Implications* these sections may have for you.

Gospel Glimpses

GRACE SUFFICIENT. The Lord tells Paul, "My grace is sufficient for you" (12:9). This promise is the heartbeat of the Christian life. Whatever pain washes into our life, his grace is sufficient. It is enough. We have him. His grace was sufficient when he first called us out of darkness into light, overcoming our natural blindness and hostility to him. His grace is sufficient now, whatever darkness we may be enveloped in. His grace will be sufficient throughout every day of our journey ahead. Whatever is subtracted from our lives through trial, disappointment, fatigue, and failure is more than made up for through the addition of his grace. To receive grace is to receive Christ. Grace is not an abstract "thing" God gives us. It is simply another way of expressing the gift of the Son to sinners. With Christ, we have enough. He is our ever-present friend, the friend of sinners, the great companion of sufferers. God's grace—in his Son—is sufficient.

Whole-Bible Connections

SUFFERING. In Eden no suffering existed. In the New Jerusalem, "Eden 2.0," no suffering will exist. But in between the first two chapters of the Bible and the last two chapters, suffering is everywhere. We see this plainly in Paul's autobiographical description of his life in 2 Corinthians 11:23–29. All humans, believers or not, suffer. But for unbelievers, suffering is hopeless, empty, vain. For believers, suffering walks us into close fellowship with Jesus, the One who came to know suffering more deeply than we ever will (Heb. 4:15). And the greatest suffering—torment in hell forever—has been wiped away from our future. One day, all our suffering will funnel into resplendence and radiance when we are with Christ in heaven. It will all turn out for our good.

STRENGTH THROUGH WEAKNESS. With the fall into sin, weakness invaded the world. Yet in his great purposes of grace, God delights to leverage weakness into his people's joy and his own glory. Throughout the Old Testament we see this theme beginning to snowball. It is when the Israelites are afflicted that they multiply all the more (Ex. 1:12). It is to Gideon, the least in his clan, that the Lord appears, calling him a "mighty man of valor" (Judg. 6:12) and using him to deliver Israel. It is young, timid Jeremiah whom God calls to exercise a prophetic ministry of international significance (Jer. 1:4–10). It is fishermen who are chosen to represent the Lord Jesus during and immediately after his earthly ministry. Paul explains clearly how weakness was the platform for divine strength in his own life and ministry (as we have seen in 2 Corinthians). And then, in the fullness of time, God himself took on weakness, the weakness of human frailty and ultimately the weakness of a cross, to bring strength and glory to his people. This principle of human weakness becoming a vessel through which God loves to display his strength is built into the way this universe runs. It is the great secret of the Christian life, the secret to joy and power. We need not run from our weaknesses or inadequacies. They are channels for *God*.

Theological Soundings

THE COSMOS. Paul says he was "caught up to the third heaven" (2 Cor. 12:2). This was a typical Jewish way of referring to the universe in terms of the immediate air around us, the sky and space above our atmosphere, and then, thirdly, the realm where God abides beyond that. Paul calls this third area "paradise" (12:3). This can sometimes refer to Eden, but more generally in the New Testament it refers to the domain of God's blessedness (Luke 23:43; Rev. 2:7). Paul experienced a glimpse of this realm of paradise for a brief time during his earthly life. Every believer will experience this paradise for an eternity in the next life.

DIVINE SOVEREIGNTY.[3] Paul says it was Satan who harassed him with the thorn in the flesh (12:7). Yet the purpose of the thorn, as Paul says twice in verse 7, was to bring Paul to a place of godly *humility*. Satan is not in the humility-generating business. So Paul clearly understood the Lord himself to be standing behind this affliction—as further evidenced by the fact that it is to the Lord that Paul addresses his request that the thorn be removed. God was the final arbiter of the events of Paul's life, both blessing and pain. Satan is indeed at work in this world for evil. Yet even Satan is not outside the bounds of God's control. Though he does not condone Satan's intents or actions, the Lord overrules every event of world history and of our own lives, great or small. Theologians thus make a distinction between God's *decretive will* (all that God decrees) and his *preceptive will* (all that God desires), explaining that the first of these is the larger wraparound category subsuming the second. There are some things that are not what the heart of God desires but that, for his own wise and good purposes, he foreordains.

Personal Implications

Take time to reflect on the implications of 2 Corinthians 11:16–12:10 for your own life today. Consider what you have learned that might lead you to praise God, repent of sin, and trust in his gracious promises. Make notes below on the personal implications for your walk with the Lord of the (1) *Gospel Glimpses*, (2) *Whole-Bible Connections*, (3) *Theological Soundings*, and (4) this passage as a whole.

1. Gospel Glimpses

2. Whole-Bible Connections

3. Theological Soundings

4. 2 Corinthians 11:16–12:10

As You Finish This Unit . . .

Take a moment now to ask for the Lord's blessing and help as you continue in this study of 2 Corinthians. And take a moment also to look back through this unit of study, to reflect on some key things that the Lord may be teaching you.

Definitions

[1] **Irony** – A literary device by which an author uses language that normally signifies its opposite, for rhetorical effect.

[2] **Satan** – A spiritual being whose name means "accuser." As the leader of all the demonic forces, he opposes God's rule and seeks to harm God's people and accuse them of wrongdoing. His power, however, is confined to the bounds that God has set for him, and one day he will be destroyed along with all his demons (Matt. 25:41; Rev. 20:10).

[3] **Sovereignty** – Supreme and independent power and authority. Sovereignty over all things is a distinctive attribute of God (1 Tim. 6:15–16). He directs all things to carry out his purposes (Rom. 8:28–29).

Week 11: A Final Pastoral Plea

2 Corinthians 12:11–13:14

▲

Paul concludes 2 Corinthians by reflecting on his imminent visit to the church at Corinth, which would be his third visit there. As he has throughout this letter, he speaks of the legitimacy of his apostolic ministry (12:14–21). He also continues to the very end his theme of strength through weakness, this time clinching this principle in the experience of Christ himself (13:4–5). Finally, Paul calls those hostile toward him to reconsider whether they truly belong to Christ (13:1–10).

The Big Picture

In 2 Corinthians 12:11–13:14 Paul launches a final plea to the Corinthian church, commending the genuineness of his ministry and calling the Corinthians to confirm the genuineness of their faith.

> ## Reflection and Discussion

Read through 2 Corinthians 12:11–13:14, the passage for this week's study. Then review the following questions, taking notes on this final section of this letter. (For further background, see the *ESV Study Bible*, pages 2239–2240; available online at esv.org.)

What are the "signs of a true apostle" (12:12)? Why would Paul appeal to these? What does this appeal imply about the work of the "super-apostles" (11:5; 12:11)?

What, according to 12:16–18, was Paul being accused of by some of the Corinthians? How does he head off this attack?

Where else in 2 Corinthians have you seen Paul say what he says in 12:19? What motive of Paul surfaces once more at the end of this verse? What must be the fundamental resource driving this motive (remember 2 Cor. 5:14–15)?

What would it mean for Paul not to find the Corinthians as he wished, and for the Corinthians not to find Paul as they wished (12:20)?

How would Paul be humbled, as he says in 12:21, in coming to Corinth? Note also Paul's reference to repentance in this verse. Remembering chapter 7, what kind of repentance/grief is Paul pursuing here?

What does Paul mean when he says he will "not spare" the Corinthian opponents when he visits (13:2)? Does this mean Paul does not, after all, wish them well (12:19)? How is this loving of Paul? As you answer, consider the way God doesn't spare (so to speak) his own children from discipline[1] (Heb. 12:5–11).

How does 13:4 cohere with the theme of 2 Corinthians as a whole, crystallized in 12:10?

Paul returns to the theme of his own weakness twice in this passage, in 13:4 and 13:9. What is the relationship between Christian weakness and Christ's weakness, according to 13:4?

What is the heart of Paul's string of exhortations closing out this letter (13:11–12)? Read John 17:20–23 as you answer. Consider your own life and reflect on what the Lord might be saying to you in light of this text.

The final verse of this letter contains the only explicitly Trinitarian benediction[2] in all of Paul's writings. What does Paul identify as the unique blessing of each person of the Trinity? How is each uniquely appropriate, given each person's role in our gracious salvation?

Read through the following three sections on *Gospel Glimpses*, *Whole-Bible Connections*, and *Theological Soundings*. Then take time to consider the *Personal Implications* these sections may have for you.

> ## Gospel Glimpses

CRUCIFIED[3] IN WEAKNESS. At the very heart of the Christian faith is the surprising historical event of a crucified Lord. This truth is "folly to those who are perishing, but to us who are being saved it is the power of God" (1 Cor. 1:18). At first glance the crucifixion of our Savior is repugnant, revolting, ludicrous, the height of ugliness. But believers recognize, to our everlasting comfort, that in his crucifixion Jesus becomes our Savior—not the Savior the Jews expected, saving them from the overlordship of pagan Rome, but the Savior we all most deeply need, saving us from the overlordship of sin and death. For he suffered in our place as a substitute, bearing the penalty we deserved. He was supremely weak on the cross—so that we, weak though we are, can one day have perfect strength restored, and can begin to enjoy that divine strength even now through the power of the Holy Spirit.

GOSPEL RELATIONSHIPS. It is a high standard to which Paul calls the Corinthians at the end of this letter. "Aim for restoration, comfort one another, agree with one another, live in peace" (13:11). Indeed, it is an impossible standard, but for the gospel! Only as we enjoy the peace with God that is ours through the atoning work of Christ can we exercise peace interpersonally. Only as we relax under the comfort Christ gives are we empowered to comfort one another—as Paul said earlier in this letter, comforting one another "with the comfort with which we ourselves are comforted by God" (1:4). One of the major messages of the New Testament is how our vertical relationship with God is meant to shape our horizontal relationships with others. The gospel of grace informs how we treat others—namely, with the grace, peace, and non-hostility with which God treats us.

> ## Whole-Bible Connections

SIGNS AND WONDERS. Paul says, "The signs of a true apostle were performed among you, . . . signs and wonders and mighty works" (12:12). Miraculous, divinely empowered signs and wonders were the attestations of a true apostle of Christ (see also Rom. 15:18–19; Gal. 3:1–5). These signs and wonders were the evidence of the work of the Holy Spirit and thus of the new covenant (Jer. 31:31–34; Ezek. 36:26). Signs and wonders were an Old Testament phenomenon too, attesting the divine favor resting on the true leaders of God's people. Throughout the Old Testament the signs and wonders surrounding the events of the exodus are remembered, leading right into the New Testament age, the age of the Spirit and the apostles (Ex. 3:20; 7:3; 10:1–2; Num. 14:22; Deut. 4:34; Josh. 24:17; Ps. 105:27–36; Acts 7:36).

DEATH. "In the day that you eat of it you shall surely die," God told Adam and Eve (Gen. 2:17). They ignored this instruction, however, and did eat of the tree of the knowledge of good and evil—and death entered into this world. The story of human history has been one of death. Every human life has ended in death and all the fear and misery that accompanies it. Every human life except one: When Jesus Christ walked out of the tomb, he signaled the defeat of death. He went through death and out the other side. We who entrust ourselves to him do indeed still die physically, but not in the most important sense. Believers in Christ have been granted, even now, eternal life (John 5:24; 6:47). The life of the age to come, the kind of life that can never be extinguished since it is life from God himself, the kind of life that raised Jesus from the dead, has washed into our lives already. And this eternal life guarantees that one day we too will be resurrected at the end of all things (John 6:54). In the new earth, "death shall be no more" (Rev. 21:4).

Theological Soundings

RESURRECTION OF CHRIST. "He was crucified in weakness, but lives by the power of God" (2 Cor. 13:4). The New Testament teaches that God the Father raised up Christ through the power of the Holy Spirit (Rom. 8:11). This was a triune act. When Jesus was raised, he was not merely resuscitated; he was not restored to corruptible life—a body that wears down, gets wrinkles, loses its hair, and so on. This was not like the raising of Lazarus. No, when Jesus was raised, he was the first instance in this exhausted world of the life of the age to come, the radiant, invincible existence every believer in Christ will one day enjoy. He was the "firstfruits," the first ingathering of the one great harvest of resurrection life for all who are united to Christ (1 Cor. 15:20–22).

UNION WITH CHRIST. The umbrella doctrine of our salvation, the broadest way of speaking of our gracious salvation, is union with Christ. When Paul exhorts the Corinthians to test whether they are truly saved, he casts this in terms of union with Christ: is it the case that "Jesus Christ is in you" (2 Cor. 13:5)? We are justified in Christ (Phil. 3:9), sanctified in Christ (1 Cor. 1:30), reconciled in Christ (Col. 1:22), raised with him (Col. 3:1), and all the rest.

TRINITY. The word *Trinity* does not appear in the Bible, but the truth of this doctrine is plainly evident when the whole of Scripture is taken into account. This doctrine was murky in the Old Testament but bursts onto the scene in the New Testament. Paul makes clear his own belief that God is triune with his closing benediction of 2 Corinthians: "The grace of the Lord Jesus Christ and the love of God and the fellowship of the Holy Spirit be with you all" (13:14). God the Father planned salvation. God the Son accomplished salvation. And God the Holy Spirit applies salvation. Grace in eternity past from the Father, grace at the climax of human history from the Son, and grace in our own present time and space from the Spirit.

Personal Implications

Take time to reflect on the implications of 2 Corinthians 12:11–13:14 for your own life today. Consider what you have learned that might lead you to praise God, repent of sin, and trust in his gracious promises. Make notes below on the personal implications for your walk with the Lord of the (1) *Gospel Glimpses*, (2) *Whole-Bible Connections*, (3) *Theological Soundings*, and (4) this passage as a whole.

1. Gospel Glimpses

2. Whole-Bible Connections

3. Theological Soundings

4. 2 Corinthians 12:11–13:14

> ## As You Finish This Unit . . .

Take a moment now to ask for the Lord's blessing and help as you continue in this study of 2 Corinthians. And take a moment also to look back through this unit of study, to reflect on some key things that the Lord may be teaching you.

Definitions

[1] **Discipline** – Pain from God as our Father for our good, motivated by his love; as distinct from pain from God as our judge for our punishment, motivated by his wrath.

[2] **Benediction** – A prayer for God's blessing at the end of a letter or a worship service. Many NT letters include a benediction.

[3] **Crucifixion** – A means of execution in which the person was fastened, by ropes or nails, to a crossbeam that was then raised and attached to a vertical beam, forming a cross (the root meaning of "crucifixion"). The process was designed to maximize pain and humiliation, and to serve as a deterrent for other potential offenders. Jesus suffered this form of execution (Matt. 27:32–56), not for any offense he had committed (Heb. 4:15) but as the atoning sacrifice for all who would believe in him (John 3:16).

Week 12: Summary and Conclusion

▲

We conclude our study of 2 Corinthians by summarizing the big picture of God's message through this letter as a whole. Then we will consider several questions in order to reflect on various Gospel Glimpses, Whole-Bible Connections, and Theological Soundings throughout the entire book.

The Big Picture of 2 Corinthians

The message of 2 Corinthians remains supremely relevant to every generation of the church. Strength comes through weakness; life through death; comfort through affliction; salvation through penitent grief.

Paul employs theological paradox throughout 2 Corinthians to upend Corinthian sensibilities influenced more by secular culture than by a cross-centered gospel. This use of paradox is so pervasive that it provides the interpretive key to the letter. Paul's short autobiographical clip recounting his "thorn in the flesh" (12:7–10), specifically his concluding statement, "When I am weak, then I am strong" (12:10), provides a hermeneutical mountaintop from which the whole of the epistle can be viewed and understood.

Confronted with the worldly outlook in Corinth—by which Christ and his apostles are being judged according to secular standards of eloquence, natural ability, and external appearance over internal reality—Paul finds himself needing to take drastic measures to show the Corinthians what authentic Christianity really is. He therefore exposes their subversively anti-Christian worldview not merely by offering a different framework, nor even by denying the accusations being fired against him, but by introducing an upside-down paradigm by which the very content of Corinthian accusation of Paul becomes the platform of apostolic confirmation.

Paul argues not only that the strength sought by the world is different from the way of the Spirit, but that true strength comes in the very thing the world shuns: weakness. In abhorring weakness, people reject the very locus of the true power they so deeply crave. In avoiding weakness, moreover, they cut themselves off from being united to Christ's weakness—and also, by necessary consequence, Christ's resurrection power.

Gospel Glimpses

We have seen clear affirmation of the gospel of grace throughout 2 Corinthians. We have seen Paul repeatedly appeal to the life, death, and resurrection of Christ as the heart of the Christian life.

Has 2 Corinthians brought new clarity to your understanding of the gospel? How so?

Were there any particular passages or themes in 2 Corinthians that led you to have a fresh understanding and grasp of God's grace to us through Jesus?

▶ Whole-Bible Connections

This letter has been rich in whole-Bible themes, as Paul affirms his own ministry as the new covenant ministry anticipated throughout the Old Testament. Paul does not explicitly quote from the Old Testament as often as in other letters such as Romans or Galatians, but the Old Testament clearly furnishes the background and the language of 2 Corinthians and Paul's view of himself and his ministry.

How has this study of 2 Corinthians filled out your understanding of the biblical storyline of redemption?

Are there any themes emphasized in 2 Corinthians that help you deepen your grasp of the Bible's unity?

Have any passages or themes expanded your understanding of the redemption that Jesus provides, begun at his first coming and consummated at his return?

What connections between 2 Corinthians and the Old Testament were new to you?

> ## Theological Soundings

Our understanding of Christian theology is greatly enriched through 2 Corinthians. Many doctrines and themes are developed, clarified, and reinforced throughout 2 Corinthians. Reflect on the doctrinal themes we have seen throughout this epistle.

Has your theology been refined at all during the course of studying 2 Corinthians? How so?

How has your understanding of the nature and character of God been deepened throughout this study?

What unique contributions does 2 Corinthians make toward our understanding of who Jesus is and what he accomplished through his life, death, and resurrection?

_____

_____

_____

_____

_____

_____

_____

_____

What specifically does 2 Corinthians teach us about the human condition and our need of redemption?

_____

_____

_____

_____

_____

_____

_____

_____

Personal Implications

God gave us the book of 2 Corinthians, ultimately, to transform us into the likeness of his Son. If our study of this letter does not strengthen our communion with God and worship of him, we have been wasting our time. As you reflect on 2 Corinthians as a whole, what implications do you see for your life?

_____

_____

_____

_____

_____

_____

_____

What life implications flow from your reflections on the questions already asked in this week's study concerning Gospel Glimpses, Whole-Bible Connections, and Theological Soundings?

What has this epistle brought home to you that leads you to praise God, turn away from sin, and trust more firmly in his promises?

As You Finish Studying 2 Corinthians . . .

We rejoice with you as you finish studying the book of 2 Corinthians! May this study become part of your Christian walk of faith, day by day and week by week throughout all your life. Now we would greatly encourage you to study the Word of God in an ongoing way. To help you as you continue your study of the Bible, we would encourage you to consider other books in the *Knowing the Bible* series, and to visit knowingthebibleseries.org.

Lastly, take a moment to look back through this study. Review the notes that you have written, and the things that you have highlighted or underlined. Reflect again on the key themes that the Lord has been teaching you about himself and about his Word. May these things become a treasure for you throughout your life—this we pray in the name of the Father, and the Son, and the Holy Spirit. Amen.